Fantastic Fairs

Traveling Carnival

by Julie Murray

Dash!
LEVELED READERS
An Imprint of Abdo Zoom • abdobooks.com

3

3 Dash!
LEVELED READERS

Level 1 – Beginning
Short and simple sentences with familiar words or patterns for children who are beginning to understand how letters and sounds go together.

Level 2 – Emerging
Longer words and sentences with more complex language patterns for readers who are practicing common words and letter sounds.

Level 3 – Transitional
More developed language and vocabulary for readers who are becoming more independent.

THIS BOOK CONTAINS RECYCLED MATERIALS

abdobooks.com

Published by Abdo Zoom, a division of ABDO, PO Box 398166, Minneapolis, Minnesota 55439. Copyright © 2020 by Abdo Consulting Group, Inc. International copyrights reserved in all countries. No part of this book may be reproduced in any form without written permission from the publisher. Dash!™ is a trademark and logo of Abdo Zoom.

Printed in the United States of America, North Mankato, Minnesota.
052019
092019

Photo Credits: Alamy, Getty Images, Granger, iStock, Shutterstock
Production Contributors: Kenny Abdo, Jennie Forsberg, Grace Hansen, John Hansen
Design Contributors: Dorothy Toth, Neil Klinepier

Library of Congress Control Number: 2018963341

Publisher's Cataloging in Publication Data
Names: Murray, Julie, author.
Title: Traveling carnival / by Julie Murray.
Description: Minneapolis, Minnesota : Abdo Zoom, 2020 | Series: Fantastic fairs |
    Includes online resources and index.
Identifiers: ISBN 9781532127274 (lib. bdg.) | ISBN 9781532128257 (ebook) |
    ISBN 9781532128745 (Read-to-me ebook)
Subjects: LCSH: Carnivals--Juvenile literature. | Attractions (Amusement rides)--
    Juvenile literature. | Fairs--Juvenile literature.
Classification: DDC 394.6--dc23

Table of Contents

Traveling Carnival

A traveling carnival is a **funfair** that moves from place to place. It is not set up at a **permanent** location. Some carnivals are set up in a parking lot.

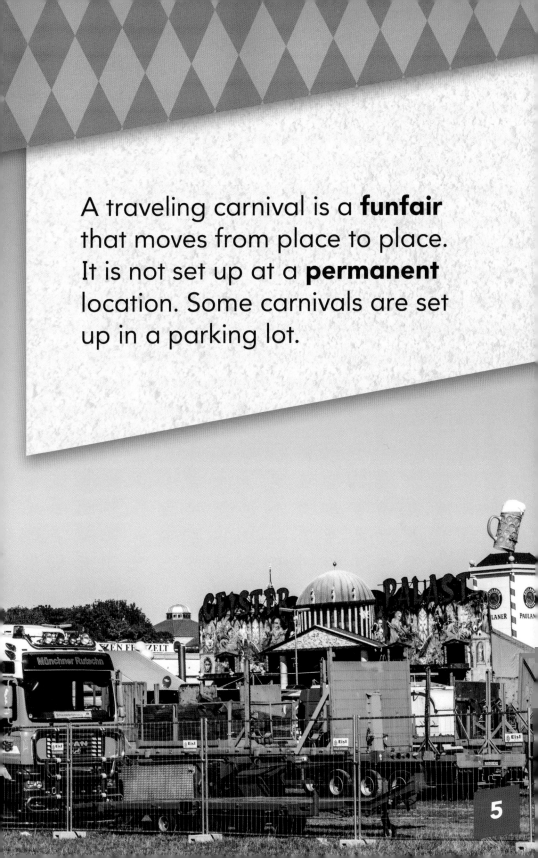

A traveling carnival has many **attractions**. There are games and rides for all ages. There is also plenty of carnival food.

EXIT

EXIT

Traveling Carnival History

The 1893 World's Fair in Chicago, Illinois, sparked the beginning of the traveling carnival. The fair had an area with food, rides, games, and **sideshows**.

This area was called the **Midway** Plaisance. This is where the term "midway" comes from.

11

After the 1893 World's Fair, traveling carnivals began touring the US. By 1937, there were more than 300 carnivals traveling around the country.

13

Back then, **sideshows** were a big part of the carnival. They had wild west shows, animal acts, and **vaudeville** performers.

15

Today's Traveling Carnivals

Today, most traveling carnivals just have games, food, and rides. Games like duck pond and balloon darts are popular. People can win stuffed animals or other prizes.

PR... EVE...
2
SPECIAL
DARTS $5.00

1 WINS SMALL
2 SMALL = MEDIUM
2 MEDIUM = LARGE
2 LARGE = JUMBO
2 JUMBO = CHOICE
E UP FOR LARGER PRIZES!

Big baby

Big baby

100 GRAND

17

There are food stands at carnivals. Funnel cakes, cotton candy, and French fries are found at traveling carnivals.

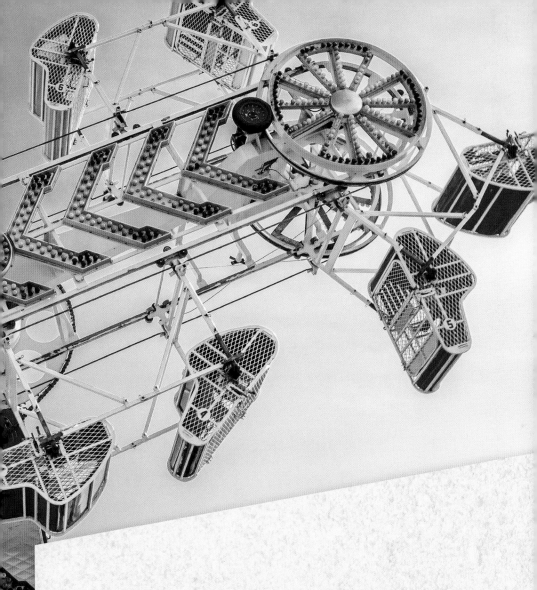

Traveling carnivals have rides for everyone. There may be a bouncy house and merry-go-round for young children. There may be a Tilt-A-Whirl and a Zipper ride for thrill seekers.

More Facts

- The Ferris wheel made its debut at the 1893 World's Fair in Chicago, Illinois. Today, it is a staple of traveling carnivals.

- It usually takes 1 to 3 days to set up a traveling carnival. It can be taken down in as little as 6 hours!

- Carnival workers spend up to 10 months on the road each year. They work long hours and often sleep in cramped living conditions.

Glossary

attractions – an event that people want to see.

funfair – a fair consisting of rides, sideshows, and other amusements.

midway – the area or strip where food stands, shows, and games are found at fairs.

permanent – lasting or meant to last for a very long time.

sideshow – a small show in addition to a main event at a fair or circus.

vaudeville – a stage show that consists of a variety of songs, dances, comic skits, and the like.

Index

Online Resources

Booklinks
NONFICTION NETWORK
FREE! ONLINE NONFICTION RESOURCES

To learn more about traveling carnivals, please visit **abdobooklinks.com** or scan this QR code. These links are routinely monitored and updated to provide the most current information available.